Quantum Dreaming

IONE

First published in 2025 by Spiral House, an imprint of Silver Press.
www.silverpress.org

ISBN: 978-1-0685918-6-0

Design by Rose Nordin
Typeset in Adobe Caslon Pro by Alice Spawls
Printed and bound in the UK by CPI

'Quantum Dreaming' © IONE
Afterword © Sarah Shin
Images © Sammy Lee

All rights reserved. No part of this publication may be reproduced, stored in a retrieval system or transmitted in any form or by any means, electronic, mechanical, photocopying, recording or otherwise, without prior permission in writing from Silver Press.

The moral rights of the authors have been asserted.

EU GPSR Authorised Representative: Logos Europe, 9 rue Nicolas Poussin, 17000, La Rochelle, France.
contact@logoseurope.eu 1 2 3 4 5 6 7 8 9 10

Contents

Quantum Dreaming — 1

Afterword — 47
    North
    by Sarah Shin

Images
    by Sammy Lee

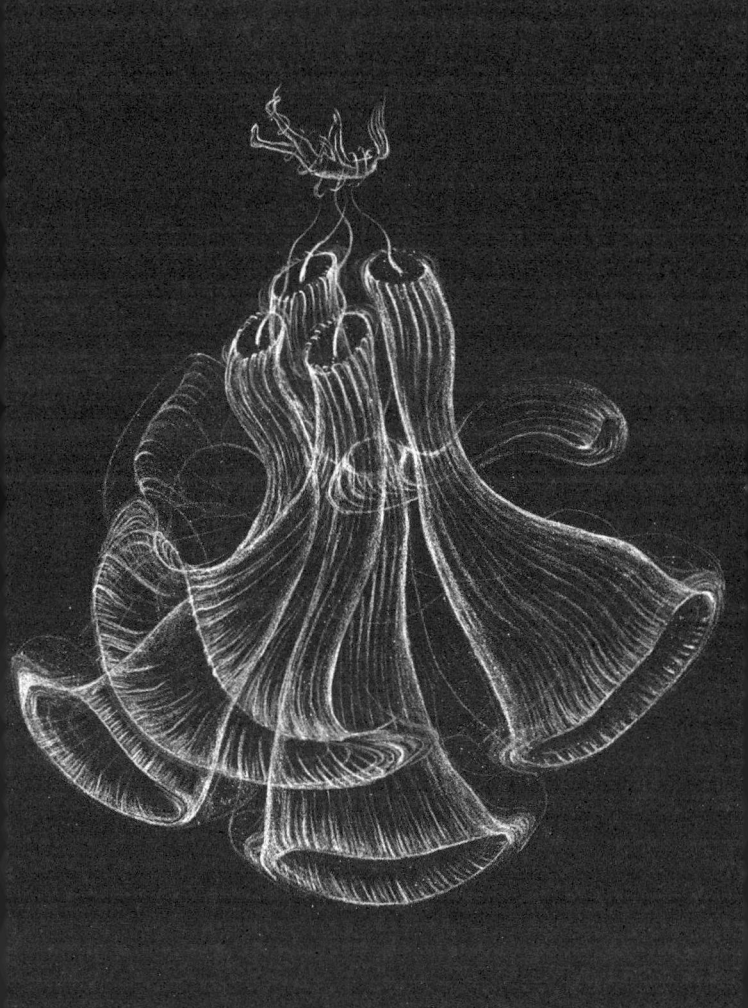

My self, my travels, my body – *my touching places on the Earth*, my receiving *blessings* from these places, my giving *blessings* back. These are, I've come to realise, milestones in the evolving process of my Quantum Dreaming.

An Illuminated Pathway

I have devoted myself and my life to dreams. I am called a Dream Keeper: a facilitator of dreams. I want to awaken others to the benefits of bringing attention to dreaming as essential to our living. I would love for all of us to experience dreams as an illuminated pathway to self-healing, one that also allows us to leave behind our current cultural limitations.

Even though dreams have been marginalised for thousands of years, we all still dream, whether we recall their content or not. Throughout my years of practising and advocating for Dream Awareness I have encouraged people to relax and have more fun with their dreams, to be curious about dream phenomena and to explore the creative aspects of dreaming. The idea is to 'lift off judgment' about our own dreams. This concept is known as 'LOJ' among many of my students and has become a reminder about our other judgments, beyond those related to dreams.

In essence, the process is truly simple. It involves becoming more aware of our dreams and moving away from linear scrutiny of dream content. Rather than analysing dreams, Dream Awareness encourages the creation of a community of dreamers. Community dreamers explore what is called 'the reality of the dream and the dream of reality'. As we share this intimate part of our being with others, we build on the ancient dream ways of those who have come before us, beginning with the dreams of our mothers and fathers, and moving back through time. Dream Awareness and sharing within the family can be a most satisfying, basic activity.

This dream philosophy is old in one sense and modern, even futuristic, in others. It is also timeless, like dreams themselves. Through freeing the dream from rigid meanings imposed by extant theories, as interesting and even helpful as they may be, we are able to explore the deep seeds of creativity located within them. We allow the waves of creativity to surface. We create poetry and texts, plays and films, dances and rituals, along with new art forms. We begin to become more aware of the needs of individuals – children, adults and elders – as well as other groups within the community.

Dreaming True

In the 1970s I spent an extended time in Spain and France. One morning, while we were living in an old stone farmhouse in the Drôme in France, my oldest son, aged two, confided in me, 'Mickey Mouse told me, hi!' I was fascinated and began to keep track of all of our dreams in my journal. I discovered that the dreams of my three young children, their father and me all contained similar themes and content. This led me to track the phenomenon elsewhere, for example in the dreams of people who lived in the same building, whether related or not. My interests over many decades have brought me to my current appreciation of the quantum nature of dreaming – that is, dreams are limitlessly interconnected over space and time.

When I returned to the US, I began facilitating dream workshops at places including the Esalen Institute in California, the Open Center in New York and my own loft, Live Letters, in downtown Manhattan. I noticed that many people I encountered were reticent or even fearful about their dreams. There was then, as there often still is now, an immediate negative response or dismissal at the very mention of dreams, such as 'I never remember my dreams'. When I began to produce city-wide Dream Festivals, one official said: 'You don't want to hear my dreams!'

In one of my regular Manhattan workshops for the Open Center, a man who had identified himself as a psychiatrist declared, 'I never dream!' There was a pause as we took this in, along with his rather defiant manner. He continued, 'And none of my patients do either.' He seemed quite proud of himself, and I felt we were all wondering why he had bothered to join this dream workshop. In retrospect, I believe he was sorely missing his dreams, and apparently could only express this in an aggressive manner. As with most declarations of this kind, the man eventually relayed something to the group – a dream from his childhood – and conceded that he, like all of us, *did* dream, and this particular dream wanted to be told.

Particularly in the early years of my teaching, I noticed that many people seemed afraid that their dreams might reveal something wrong with them. I attribute that to the marginalisation of dreams for centuries, along with the demonisation of women and all cultures of colour. This has

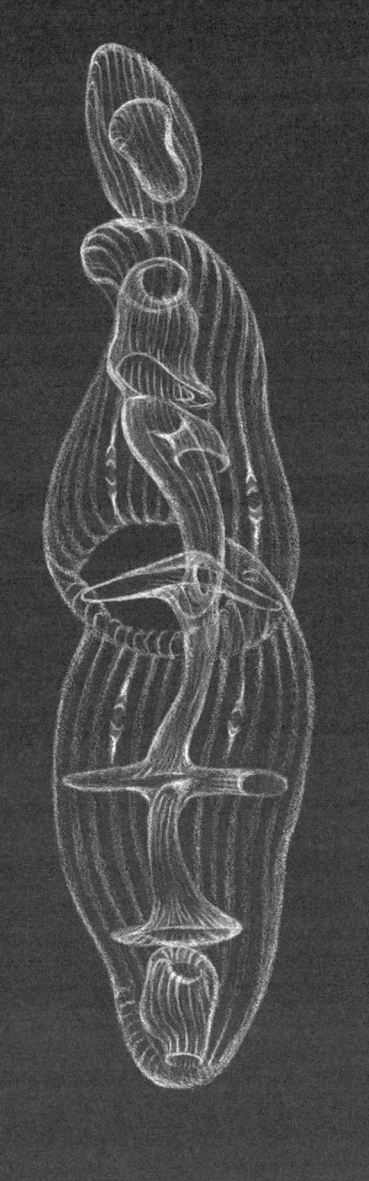

been helped along in modern times by the wide dissemination of Freudian dream interpretations.

I believe Dream Awareness can reveal what's *right* about us and the world around us. That is, we can begin to recognise and understand our own symbols, dream themes and deep feelings through the simple yet truly profound practice of paying attention. As we begin to appreciate their subtleties and share them more directly with our families and friends, we create a Dream Community that has many life-affirming properties.

A few tenets emerged during my workshops:

1. *We can learn 'full body listening'.* We can 'receive' a dream from the person telling it as a feeling or a sensation. If we are still and listen quietly, we can listen with the body to the subtle or overt 'true feeling' of the dream. It can also be received from groups of people.

2. *Our dreams can hold more than one meaning at a time*, and be considered through the lens of any dream methodology, according to what feels meaningful and helpful at any given time. We don't let interpretation take over our entire relationship with our dreams, but allow them their own ontological integrity. We could say that we free our dreams by allowing for several levels of communion with them.

3. *Dreams are multisensory experiences.* Since our dreams tend to be visually evocative, captivating us in a filmic manner, we often overlook the other sensory elements at play. The riches of sound, touch and taste are available in many dreams as we pay more attention.

4. *Dreams are accompanied by what I call Dreaming True, which relates to the truthful access to feelings.* These feelings accompany the stories of our dreams or their essential content. While the fanciful or surreal elements of the stories themselves may be initially confusing, I suggest that we can count on the truth of the feelings to provide basic information about aspects of ourselves that are not always readily accessible to us because they have been submerged and squelched from childhood onwards. It is important to note that the true feelings entailed are those within the field of the dream, rather than outside it.

5. *When one person is telling another a dream, the other person is experiencing their own version of that dream.* In sharing, they are automatically communicating on a deep feeling level, whether or not they understand the stories and symbolism. Hence, beauty and harmony can result in a Dream Community where the feelings of others are known and respected.

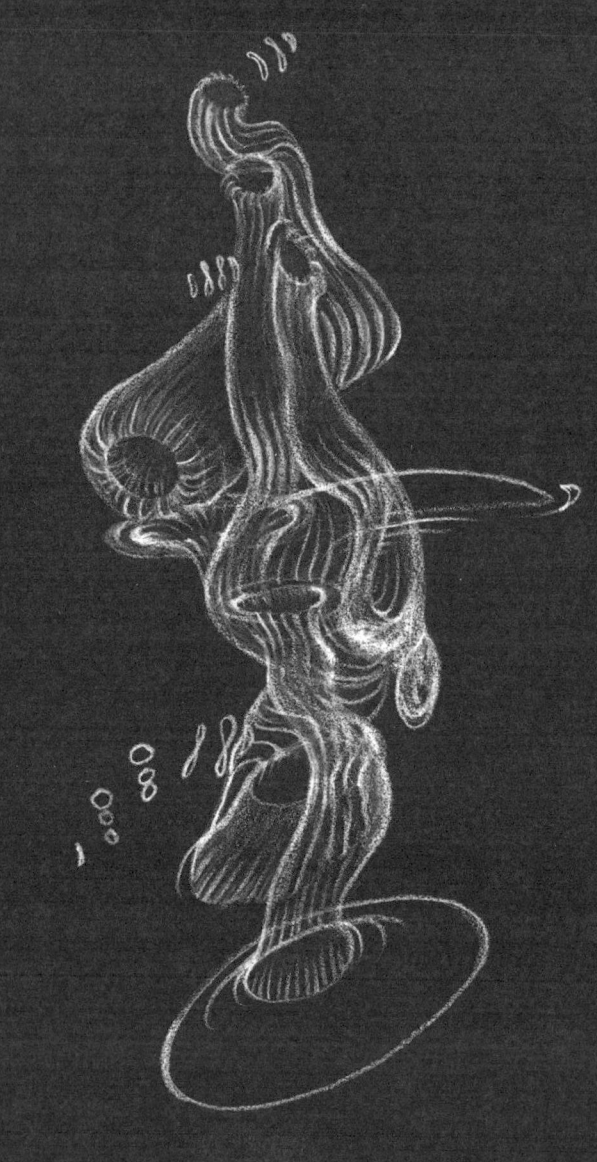

For me, dreams are never disappointing. They are always a unifying force, when shared. They have an uncanny way of breaking down barriers with ease, awakening 'aha moments' in individuals and whole groups of people. I've enjoyed sharing the unique good feelings that expand through rooms in which endorphin-releasing dreams have been expressed. The following dream, featuring oceans and mammalian sea creatures, is fairly archetypal:

I am somewhere by the ocean. Up on huge cliffs. I think it is a look-out point. There is a small crowd. Then, suddenly, whales start breaching out of the ocean. They are almost flying! I think they are humpbacks. It is so beautiful. I am aware of the cliffs and the vastness of the ocean. I am a little uneasy from it but it is also somehow very serene. The sun is setting. Lots of purple and blue water colour throughout.

The feelings transmitted by a dream like this can be powerful, and are retrievable for years. What a gift it is to access embodied feeling, free of intellectualising judgment.

Dreams are holographic. Over time I realised that when people say they don't have dreams, they are most often expecting to experience a 'complete story'. I champion fragments as important phenomena because they are capable, when amplified, of being 'holographic' and yielding important results about the whole system of the dream from the smallest bit of information.

Consider the torus of the heart – the electromagnetic field that holographically extends twelve to thirteen feet from the body.[1] Earth is at the centre of such a holographic field. We seem to live in a nested grouping of toroid energy systems that extend from atom to human to planet to solar system, out to the galaxy, and beyond that to the far reaches of the universe.

The Big Dream

The Big Dream is the great mystery from which we come. I distinguish it from our individual night-time and day dreams, though I believe it embraces them all. Images arise in my mind, influenced by this cosmic dream. I love to hear about the universe, the multiverse, black holes and white holes. The stars and entire galaxies, birthing and dying out there, punctuating the darkness – it is an extraordinary display.

We can only detect five per cent of the matter in the universe. 'Dark matter' and 'dark energy' are the names given to the other ninety-five per cent, a mysterious mass-energy that is invisible, even undetectable, to us but that must be there for the part we can detect to make sense. Though the use of the term 'dark' is evocative, betraying our age-old fears and fascinations, dark matter does not have any relation to light; it does not emit, reflect or even absorb it. Light of all types seems to pass through it as though it is completely transparent. We infer its existence from its gravitational effects on galaxies: dark matter binds galaxies together.

Meanwhile, dark energy is the force which drives the cosmic expansion. We can observe light coming from galaxies that are billions of light-years away, including the Cosmic Microwave Background (CMB), the oldest detectable light in the universe. Its faint, diffuse glow permeates the cosmos. This ancient radiation, which scientists say is a remnant from the universe's early years – around 380,000 years after the Big Bang – offers a snapshot of the universe's infancy. The CMB is visible at a distance of 13.8 billion light-years in all directions from Earth, leading scientists to posit that this is the true age of the observable universe.

However, the universe itself may be far larger than this. In the 1920s, astronomers including Edwin Hubble discovered that galaxies seem to be moving away from us, and the farther they are, the faster they are receding. In 1998, two independent groups of researchers found that this expansion is accelerating much faster than previously thought. This puzzling accelerated expansion is attributed to dark energy.

The further away a galaxy is from us, then, the faster it is moving – to a point where distant stars are moving so fast that their light will never reach us. This creates what is known as the cosmic event horizon, beyond which everything is unknowable.

I am intrigued by the preponderance of what we are not yet seeing – what we do not know. Imagine adding the possibility of other ways of 'knowing' to the exclusive form of science that has dominated Westernised cultures for centuries. I sense there is something within and beyond all of the discoveries of our cosmic lenses. The something is what I'm calling the Big Dream and it too, is invisible – yet it makes itself known, here, there and everywhere! It infuses our nighttime dreaming and punctuates our day dreams as well, as if trying to 'get our attention'.

It has many names among many cultures. Dream messages are commonly sought and received and documented throughout history, all noted and preserved in the Bible, the Qur'an, the Torah and Kabbalah teachings. The Dreaming is the Australian Aboriginal name describing a force within all things that connects past, present and future. The Dreaming informs the Aboriginal people's relationship with the land, the environment, and with all sentient beings. The Big Dream also has a kinship to the Dao, the ancient Chinese philosophy and way of being. The Dao is an elusive, ever-present force that transcends ordinary understanding and verbal expression. As the *Daodejing* says, 'The Dao that can be spoken is not the Eternal Dao.'

For physicist Fred Alan Wolf, there is a connection between The Dreaming (Dream Time) and what is termed 'quantum potential', the tendency or urge that makes our very existence 'happen'.[2] According to Wolf, both quantum physics and Aboriginal spiritual practices describe a reality that is not fixed but is instead a field of limitless potential and interconnectedness. Consider this possibility: the quantum physical universe exists as pure potential. When we observe it, we select out of that potential to create our experience.

Wolf and Arnold Mindell, who teaches in the fields of physics and psychology, see The Dreaming as an expression of the same limitless potential and interconnectedness described by quantum physics. They see the connection between ancient spiritual understanding and modern quantum theory. The non-local nature of quantum potential points to the idea that our consciousness could be connected to the very fabric of the universe.

The 'message' of all these forces is mostly inexpressible and primarily non-verbal, but if there were words, I feel a translation might be: 'Something is happening and you are an integral part of it. You and all your family and acquaintances – you and all those objects and beings who appear in your individual dreams, both waking and sleeping.'

Night dreams, wispy day dreams and many levels of trance states that we may be familiar with are all a part of my definition of 'dreaming'. It is an expanded definition: I include what mainstream researchers sometimes call hallucinations, hypnopompic and hypnagogic states – those cushiony, pliable mental states that occur between waking and sleeping. We may be paying little quality attention to these states. We brush them away, saying 'it was only a dream' and not worthy of attention. Mindell suggests that when we ignore these subtle states, and the messages and visions comprising them, we lose essential parts of who we are.

I propose that through fine-tuning our attention and expanding our awareness of our various types of dreams, our own creator/creation role within the Big Dream can become more accessible to us. We might go from feeling like something is missing, to a sense of greater meaning. Through Dream Awareness, which incorporates all the

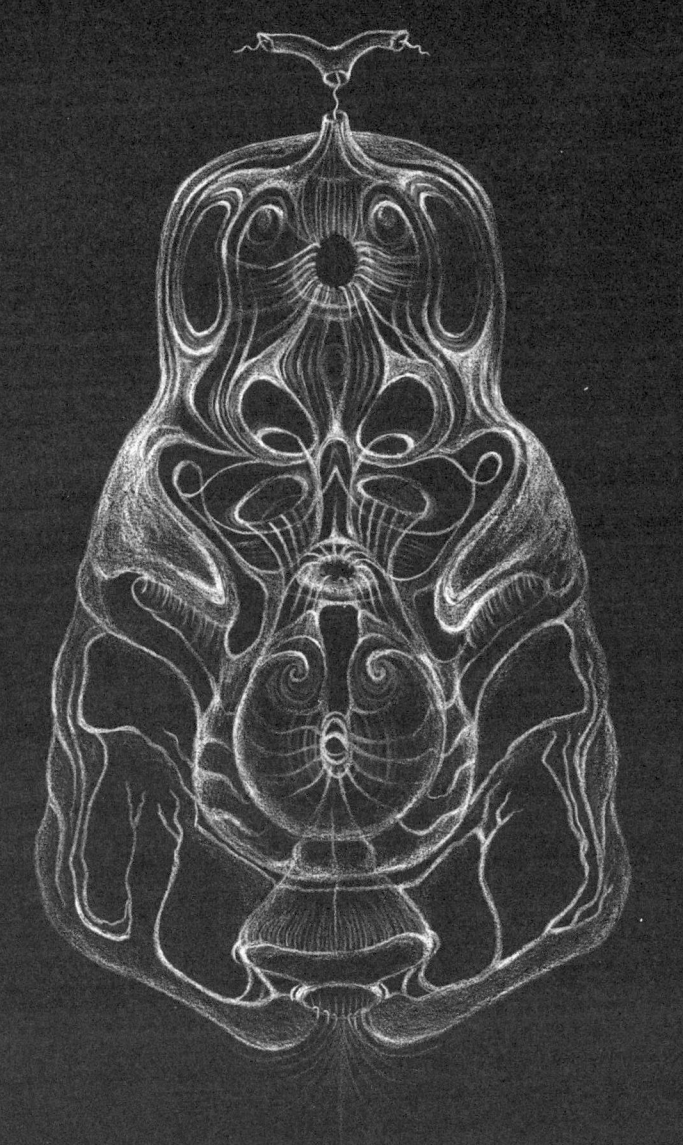

forms of dreaming mentioned above, all the way up to the Big Dream that holds them all, I'm suggesting we can lead more authentic lives.

Activities of secular and spiritual provenance like yoga, qi gong and all the martial arts have become mainstream. These practices are trying to assist us to recover a lost sense of wholeness. Yet, for the most part, what might be called Enlightenment – truly waking to 'what there is' – eludes us.

Dream Awareness may be an unexpected vehicle to lead us there, but I find it is the allure of the Big Dream message that sustains me.

Listening in Dreams

Over time I have observed several forms of listening in dreams. They include listening to recognisable voices, such as friends, family and deceased close relatives and friends; listening to unknown voices, often an impartial speaker shortly before rising; listening to conversations within a dream story context; and listening to one's own voice speaking or crying out. Sometimes, listening in dreams involves receiving the information of people conversing through a form of 'sonic telepathy'; having the memory of sounds within a dream;

or listening to the sound of one's own thoughts. Music also appears as 'ear worms' during sleep and waking and the dreamer may compose or receive new music, a spiritual song, sound, mantra or important life message while dreaming or upon awakening in a hypnopompic state. External sounds can also enter the dream, often taking on and blending with one's own story content, while sometimes dreamers listen to and speak a foreign language (an existing language or a dream-invented language) and understand it perfectly.

Listening in dreams points to the relationship between consciousness and dreams – a complex, widely studied and debated area in neuroscience, psychology, and philosophy. We know that consciousness and dreaming share neural mechanisms. Studies have shown that many of the brain regions involved in conscious experience are also active during dreaming. This suggests that dreams are allied with what is called consciousness as a kind of altered state. Similarly, dreams seem entangled with memory.

Dreaming is connected with the Rapid Eye Movement (REM) stage of sleep, deprived of which we quickly decline physically and mentally. After decades of speculation, exciting new research is helping us to understand the reason why we dream in the first place. Dream researchers have always been puzzled by the fact that babies and most animals exhibit REM sleep in the womb, as well as in infancy and beyond.

Professor Marc Blumberg, Chair of the Department of Psychological and Brain Sciences at the University of Iowa, studied twitches during sleep. Humans have been concerned for millenia by sleep or dream paralysis, in which sleepers are unable to move their bodies, apart from their eyes which perform a kind of twitching. Blumberg arrived at the understanding that twitches are signals, indicating that we are in the process of learning and in some cases repairing the territory of our bodies. The twitches are the means by which the body is communicating with the brain.

The recognition of the 'twitch factor' in humans and animals, from gestation and beyond, confirms the idea that there is no disconnect between the body and the brain during dream time despite the slowing down of muscle activity. This will also assist with the development of healing processes concerning both brain and body. In essence, the brain is listening to the body and the dream is their communication.

The quantum theory of consciousness suggests that it can exist everywhere simultaneously. Your own consciousness can be entangled with others' across vast distance. This controversial theory challenges classical models that rely solely on standard neural activity, and was first posited in the early 1990s by Nobel laureate for physics Roger Penrose, and anaesthesiologist Stuart Hameroff. A team of Wellesley College researchers led by Professor Mike Wiest supports this theory. The team gave rats a drug that binds to microtubules – tiny structures inside neurons – and found that the rats took longer to become unconscious when given anaesthesia. They surmised that the anaesthesia bound to these microtubules, slowing down the onset of unconsciousness, proving that consciousness is generated within them.

Living the Quantum Dream

Enduring sensations and feelings such as those that come down through time to us from our ancestors, or the strong presences we notice in certain structures or locations of nature, are expressions of dreaming revealing our inherent quantum nature.

I still see the ancient Egyptian, and later the Greek, pilgrims arriving at Saqqara to sleep and dream beside the Step Pyramid. I've walked that sand and listened to subliminal sounds of dreaming spirits there, where they would petition the priestess or priest. The feelings of their beliefs

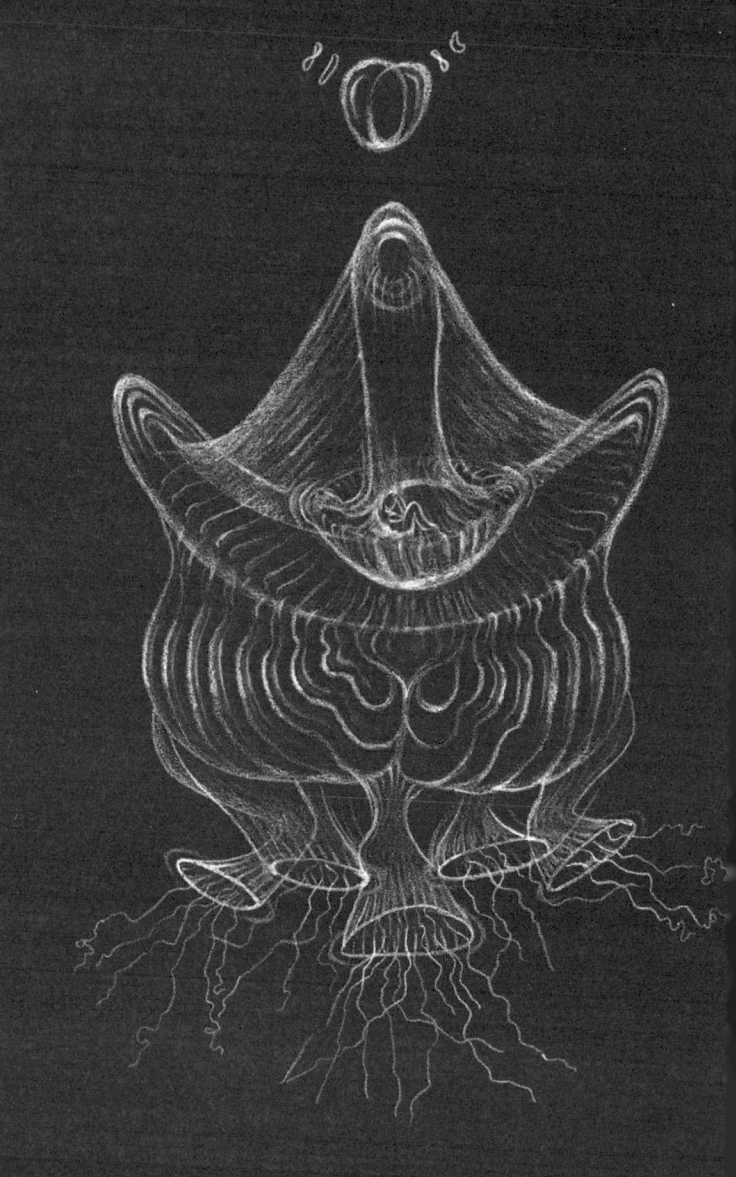

and their need for their dreams resonate even today.

Imhotep is credited with designing the Step Pyramid of Djoser, the first pyramid rising in steps, in around 2780 BCE. The great architect, magician and physician was deified by the ancient Egyptians, and was said to come to sleeping dreamers in the guise of a black canine or a snake. During a brief time of studying hieroglyphics in the 1990s, I noted thousands of snake images throughout the texts, with both positive and negative connotations. There were cults of the skin-shedding snake that revered its healing properties, both symbolically and through dream-inducing potions of venom. In even earlier times, healers' abodes bore flags with images of snakes, symbols of regeneration.

In early 2012, I was travelling in Spain along the Mediterranean Coast. A few kilometres north of Girona, I came across the stone ruins of an Asclepieion sanctuary, dedicated to the mythic healer Asclepius. The ancient city of Empuries hosted a thriving community of dreamers there between 400 and 200 BCE. A dream-like energy lingers there still. Pauline Oliveros, my partner and travelling companion, found a shady spot to rest and perhaps to dream in the extreme heat, while I wandered the grounds, gazing at the time-worn stones. I pondered the statue of this long-ago teacher, whose practices included sleep and dream sessions with attendants incorporating a variety of medicinal plants, oils, psychotropic potions and live snakes.

Asclepius, born of Apollo and a human, was instructed in medical practices by the centaur Chiron, establishing the roots of medicine, surgery and pharmacology, building on the work of earlier healers such as Imhotep. The cult of Asclepius spread throughout the Mediterranean for thousands of years after the rituals at the Pyramid of Saqqara, with participants performing rituals, processions and performances in ongoing festivals. Dream Awareness was an integral part of the early development of medical practices. Incubation, termed *Enkoimesis* by the Greeks, was a form of 'temple sleep' that may have involved hypnodelic elements to access altered states of consciousness. At the Asclepieion, after purification and making offerings, seekers would sleep in the Abaton, the dream incubation chamber. There, they hoped to receive healing or oracular dreams from Asclepius to guide their therapeutic treatment by the temple's physician-priests. This is a process the participants in my circles continue to explore. We dream overnight, or over several nights when possible, seeking guidance and healing information, or spontaneous healing for ourselves or another. Building upon ancient traditions, we can call upon a powerful wisdom figure to assist.

The Caduceus symbol of modern medicine shows a snake (or two snakes) winding round a staff, a reference to Asclepius. In some paintings, care is taken to represent him with a dog. He is holder of the older, less well-known, Egyptian practices of Imhotep and subsequent leaders and priests in Saqqara at the Step Pyramid complex, where archaeologists continue to unearth remarkable new findings.

Before moving permanently to the Hudson Valley of New York, I stayed in a rented house there. Dreaming with students during the night, I was visited by 'a wise being' whom I did not recognise. *He sweeps his arms out and I see the entire city spread out before me, with its many church steeples rising high. I hear his words: 'You will settle in this town.'* A year or so later I met and recognised this figure of wisdom in the physical healing form of a gifted holistic practitioner in a nearby town. When I shared the dream with him, he was delighted to have played such a dream role in my life. I have been 'settled' in this town for thirty-five years now.

*

Incubation spells were numerous among the Egyptians and the Greeks. A typical spell would have involved dipping a reed in myrrh or another special substance and writing on clean papyrus. Incense might be burned, and the space and dreamer herself would be purified by applying special essential oils. The papyrus might then be placed under a lamp or under a pillow. Certain phrases would be repeated a certain number of times – three or seven were popular – then a deity would be invoked to oversee her dream request. This ancient system adapts well to our modern times.

I love the concept of the 'dream temple', which proliferated in Ancient Egypt and Greece, and often give this title to my workshops for those who are interested in this aspect of dreaming. You could create your own private dream temple in your bedroom, starting by clearing away any distracting elements. Instead, fill the room and your mind with thoughts that represent the best of what you want for yourself and the world. You could imagine benevolent beings around you or think of a beloved grandmother, or read soothing words before sleep.

In many Native traditions, a creative endeavour is always dreamed before it is created in this reality. Many artists use their dreams as inspiration for new work, for dreams are our deepest source of creativity: many avid dreamers receive answers to tough problems, or find new creative resources.

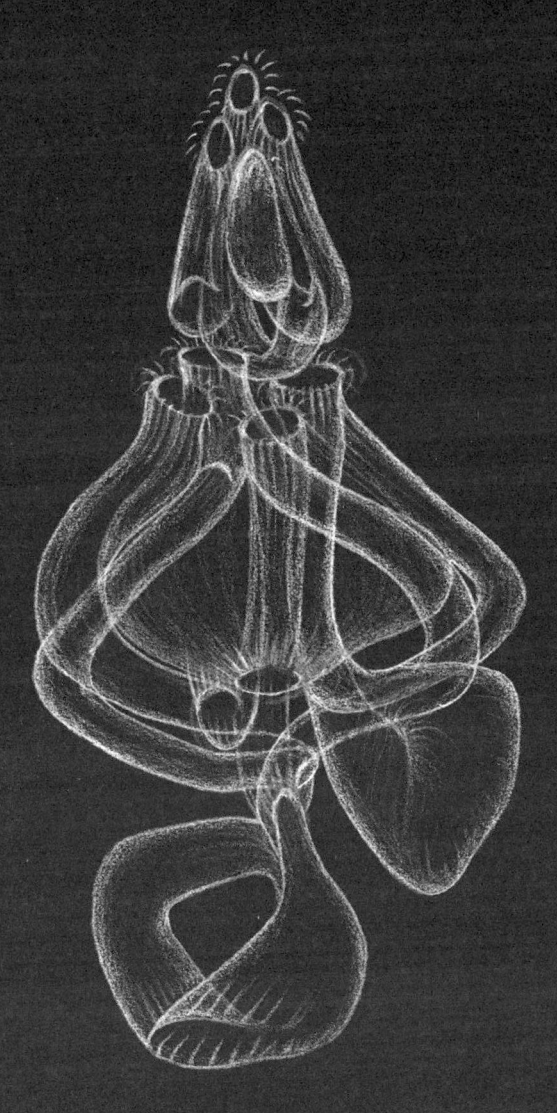

Dreaming Messages

During the seventeenth century, Njinga Mbandi (a contemporary of English Queen Elizabeth I) was the queen-king of the Mbundu kingdoms of Ndongo and Matamba in present-day Angola. She listened to her forebears through their bones, carried by her warriors into each of her battles against the colonising Portuguese. The dreaming messages and directives emanating from the bone box gave tactical advice that ensured Njinga would be victorious. Her reign lasted for forty years, and Angola was never free after her death until 1975, when the Portuguese withdrew. Dreaming back to Njinga, I researched and set forth her life, and her encounter with the Europeans: first with her father as a child, and later accompanied by the bones. Staged in 1993 at Brooklyn Academy of Music's Next Wave Festival, my stage bone box is now in my meditation room, and seems to retain some of Njinga's inherited power.

I have been inspired by the stories that have come to us of the Dream Festivals of the Haudenosaunee people, who were called Six Nations or Iroquois by British and French settlers, who dwelled close to where I live now in the Hudson Valley of New York. During these festivals, rowdy games included guessing the dreams of participants. What was interpreted as a 'dream soul' was expressing its needs in each dream. It was auspicious to find out just what its needs were and to attempt to provide this for the dreamer.

These dreams and visions inspired my own international Annual Dream Festivals, begun in 1995, and earlier gatherings, begun in the 1980s, in New York City at my loft and at Joseph Papp's Public Theater. Creative dream activities, storytelling, dream sharing, spontaneous and improvisational Dream Action theatre, music, painting and more are all featured throughout a year of celebrating our dreams. But one of the important aspects of the Festivals was to reach unsuspecting targets, who didn't value their dreams but who began to pay more attention simply through hearing about it all.

The Esopus people, a subgroup of the Lenape (or Delaware) people, continue their lives in my own dreaming, especially when I am close to the Esopus River, a few minutes away from my home. I have received, as well, the dreams of the nineteenth-century African burial ground discovered and unearthed in Lower Manhattan prior to my writing about Njinga Mbandi. I sense that they are, in some way, with me. I have come to understand this 'sensing' or feeling as an attribute of my being a part of the Big Dream.

Dreams also brought Lakota Sioux chief, Mary Elizabeth Thunder, Reverend of the Blue Star Church, and me together for several years of work and high rituals at her Texas ranch, in Italy, and in ancient temples in Egypt. Thunder's dreaming revealed a past life story that needed completion. One way to complete it was to go to the source of the story and seek resolution.

Whenever there was not a raging war in the region, I had been able to take my students to Egypt to experience the deep dreaming of the land, to experience the sound in the temples, to lift voices and meditate within the paws of the Sphinx, to float on the Nile in graceful felucca sail boats.

During my subsequent trip to Egypt (there would be nine in total), all of this and more was experienced with Thunder, her warriors and her students. I went with my own priestess, Reverend Andrea Goodman. We performed rituals in the temples, sang and chanted. We danced Peace Dances by the Nile, which also included local Egyptians. And after our journey, Thunder's dream story gradually came to completion.

The Middle of the Night

It was the middle of the night, 2014, in Kingston, and I was steeped in my books, ready to depart for Venice with Pauline, when I was overcome by feelings. I had just read of the important moment that united Venice and Egypt. I wanted to make this historical journey from Venice to Alexandria. I would trace this trip with the sure knowledge of the dream. I would claim my opera, the writing, and all the research. I would understand that the ancient journey by boat was still possible, but these days would involve flight.

Arriving in Cairo after a heady Venetian residency, we would be met by sixteen students and taken along the Nile on a boat called the *Afendena*. Pauline would take a swift trip back to the US for her students. Our friends were Zakaria, composer/designer of El Mastaba, a collaborator; and Zizo, a composer with his voice and magical oud.

Zakaria sent us, years later, many of his poems:

> Birds of skies, birds of prairies, winged friends
> Voices of joyous dawn, mesmerising sounds of dusk
> Messengers and migrators of Mother Earth
> Inspirational, devotional by their chants and calls
> Ornament of trees and ground, colouring skies and dunes
> Be with us, share with us your wisdom and voice of our ancestors

By 2017, Pauline had joined me in the dream. I had glimpsed the Flowers of the Island. We had opened the show: *The*

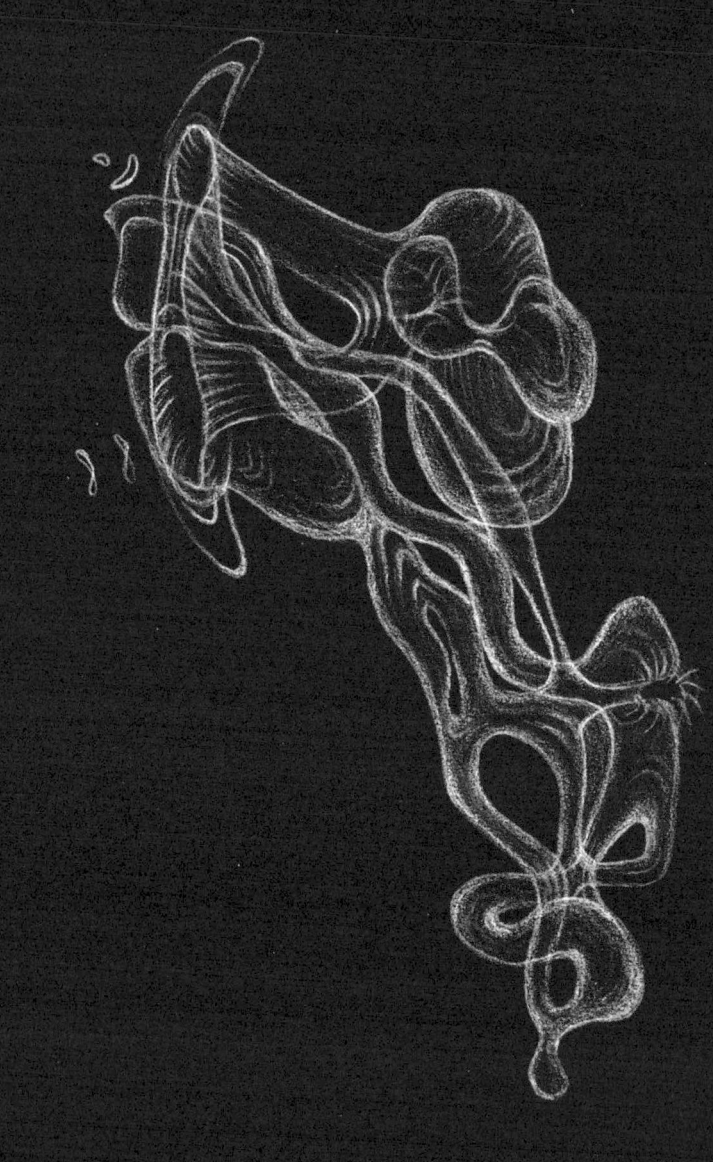

Nubian Word for Flowers, an opera.

A Dream of Pauline

As we've seen, the quantum theory of consciousness suggests that consciousnesses can be entangled over great distances. I believe this can and does occur through dreams.

While writing this manuscript, I noticed that an email had come into my inbox entitled 'A Dream'. I was stunned to receive a message from a friend of Pauline and me, who lives in Italy. In her dream, she was walking with Pauline on a beach.

'IONE is fine,' Pauline says, 'but when she loses herself on the computer, she forgets to eat.'

I was astounded. Though it was not the first time Pauline had communicated with me over distance – in this case through dimensions via another's dream – this message was particularly meaningful. I felt it was a direct support for me, demonstrating the quantum nature of dreams by transcending past, present and future.

Pauline was always known for her compassion for those who were grieving, making sure that they had necessities such as food – she would often cook big pots of chicken soup, for example. To give further weight to this message, I admit I had found it challenging to feed myself well, ever since I was no longer cooking for two, and this dream was a direct reference to that as well.

Communicating through others' dreams is a particularly community-based choice. Pauline and I had, since we first met, explored various aspects of consciousness, including oracular forms and intuitive visioning with each other, and she was a prime support for me in these investigations. 'I believe in oracle forms,' she wrote, in a journal in the 1970s, a decade before we met.

Terms such as 'telepathy' or 'mind-reading' are aspects of our dreaming, and they are integral to human experience. This kind of communication has always been present in the ongoing groups I facilitate, becoming more and more noticeable the longer we are together. Whether in person or at vast physical distance from each other, online, the community of dreamers begin to notice elements of each other's imagery and feelings and topics seeping in. In addition, themes and ideas often make themselves known even before the group meets. A dreamer can, without realising it, have 'a dream for the whole group' that addresses a mutual need.

Dream Communities

Through the ages and throughout the world, people meet, often sitting together in a circle in a long house or a tipi, sometimes around a meal, sometimes around a fire. This may take place on regularly established occasions, perhaps at a sacred spot in the woods. People take time to express what is on their minds and in their hearts.

For example, the Maori of New Zealand continue to sleep and dream together in marae, sacred structures that continue and reinforce their traditions. The Aboriginal people of Australia continue their profound relationship to dreams and to the wisdom and spirit inherent to The Dreaming or Dream Time, gathering and communing with teachers at sacred locations on the land. The potential for learning from our dream states is profound.

Jesse Little Star Baird, a teacher residing in Connecticut, reclaimed her people's long-forgotten Wôpanâak language through careful attention to her visions. In a sequence of visions, which she distinguished from night-time dreaming but which I (as I explained to her) include under the umbrella of 'dreaming' alongside a range of trance states, she observed several circles of Native American people. Each vision was clearer than the last, beginning with recognising a member of her people, then hearing a group, whom she recognised as part of her family, chanting words. Not long after, she was driving on Cape Cod and saw the sign for Sippewissett. She had seen this sign before, but this time she had a kind of epiphany that this was her language. Through being attuned to her visions, Jesse eventually reclaimed the entire Wôpanâak language enough to teach it to others. 'It was like I hadn't eaten for a long time and I had to have it to survive,' she said. Her efforts were vital to the reconstruction of her people's language and to Indigenous language preservation efforts.

I believe Dream Communities are capable of ushering in a revolution through gentle perseverance. This is such a strong claim that some wonder how serious I am. Yet, I feel it is already underway. Because it is a slow endeavour and subtle, it may not receive the attention of other more easily advertisable causes. I don't mind this, as I feel the concept is lurking in the psyche and will, one day, emerge in its full form. I call what I'm proposing a 'soft revolution' because it is not overt. This kind of revolution has a softness to it that nonetheless has a satisfying power. It is power from within, as opposed to 'power over'.[3]

The goal of the revolution is to encourage a state of being

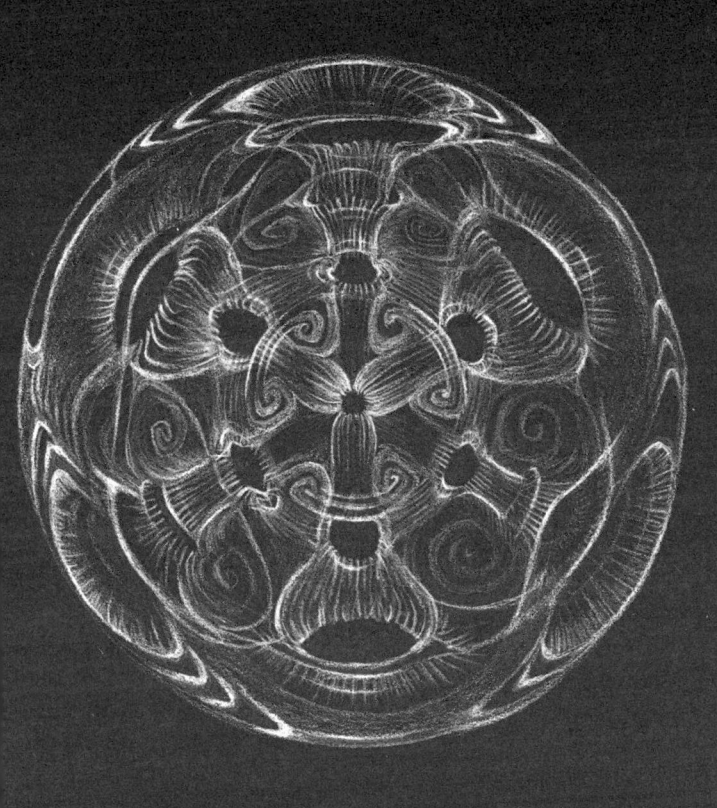

human in which violence is no longer appealing or necessary.

I feel that incorporating radical awareness of dream states can effectively curtail what some researchers have called the attrition of our consciousness. Studies have shown a steep decline in cross-linkages in the brain networks, causing sensory synthesis and associative thinking to be reduced. The research claims that consciousness is becoming more limited. Our brains are processing more and more information, and less of it is reaching consciousness.[4]

'Perception and awareness may not be located only inside of us,' writes physicist Arnold Mindell. 'The source of life itself does not reside within one particular body but is a shared, entangled experience involving all of us, the environment, and anything and everything in the universe.'[5] Our dreaming extends beyond our bodies over distance in a similar manner.

Shining light on our dream states can mean the start of a new way of being with each other. I believe we are actually interacting with each other on a dream level all the time without always being aware of it. The subtle sensations, both psychological and physical, that we feel from others, are not imagination, but have real communicative aspects. Invisible pheromones affect us on hormonal levels, such as the attraction between lovers, or the antipathy toward certain individuals. The synchronisation of menstrual cycles among women has been recorded in college dorms and among women spending time in other kinds of proximity to each other. Perhaps we once used such skills more overtly. I believe we can begin to consider this skill to be a part of our inborn 'Dream tool-kit'. Perhaps, we dreamers can bring about the shift in consciousness that creates a harmonious World Wide Quantum Dream Community.

Give Us Back Our Dreams!

Leonard Schlaine, in *The Alphabet Versus the Goddess*, points to the invention of the printing press as a kind of 'perfect storm'. He postulates that the rise of alphabetic literacy is correlated with a shift from right-brain dominance, with its association with imagery and dreaming, to the left-brain linear activity of writing and reading, creating a cerebral imbalance. In the wake of these and other historical factors, our understanding of ourselves as part of a single dreaming universe was lost. This shift was accompanied by intense violent propensities, both physiological and psychological. Millions of women, whose lives and healing practices involved earth reverence and familiarity with herbal and psychotropic remedies, were hunted and burned as witches. This remains a haunting genetic memory for many women, contributing to ongoing fear and pain.

When I began my in-depth work with women's groups throughout the 1970s and 80s, I realised that though what has been called the second wave of the women's movement had created some kinds of 'liberation', there was still plenty to be done in a world where women were still second-class citizens. I realised that women still needed to reclaim their capacity to *dream big* including and beyond social, structural, economic and political systems.

On 24 June 2022, the US Supreme Court overturned the constitutional right to an abortion, reversing the 1973 *Roe v. Wade* ruling which had granted women this right up until about twenty-four weeks' gestation. Such recent legal decisions underline how patriarchal belief systems still seek to control women's bodies. Meanwhile, we are seeing the disturbing effects of continuing colonialism and extractive capitalism in the form of worldwide violence, genocide, poverty and sickness.

This ongoing subjugation has contributed to a steep rise in opioid addictions and suicide rates, spreading from populations of colour to upper middle class and white children and adults. Addiction flows from a desire to fill the void left by the loss of the deep creativity and authentic sense of self inherent in our connection to the Big Dream.

Once we start practising awareness, our consciousness becomes more self-aware. We begin to relate to each other as more fully evolved humans, revealing to ourselves and to others the fuller capabilities we have as Quantum Dreamers within the Big Dream.

Quantum Dreaming

The Quantum Dreamer seeks to bring awareness to the omnipresence of our dream states as conscious communication across time and space.

The Quantum Dreamer seeks elimination of the appeal of violence.

The Quantum Dreamer seeks to free herself and others from enslavement.

The Quantum Dreamer recognises the common threads between the subjugation of women, the subjugation of ethnic groups by genocide or slavery, and the subjugation of the non-human natural world.

As a quantum link to the Big Dream, this means nothing

less than expanding what I consider to be our limited definitions of the word 'dream'.

And along the way, since dreams are intricately entangled with it, the work of Quantum Dreaming is to expand our consciousness itself.

Epilogue: On Rose Mountain

I have always enjoyed exploring taste, touch, and particularly *sound* in dreams. I was able to deepen these explorations during the Deep Listening Retreats on Rose Mountain, New Mexico, launched in 1991 with Pauline and Tai Chi and Movement Specialist Heloise Gold. These retreats marked the beginning of twenty-seven years of the three of us teaching together and were the manifestation of a shared vision rooted in the Big Dream.

During our very first serious conversation together in a country house in the Hudson Valley in 1982, Pauline and I found ourselves sharing our visions for the future. We realised we had the very same dream. Later that evening, out on the porch, we saw a shooting star. Only through a deep consciousness dive can I locate the place in myself that foresaw that we would live this dream together for thirty-four years and more to come.

We both saw a harmonious, self-sustaining network of artists and performers sharing their creations with each other and with the world. We saw a community of like-minded dreamers, able to support their art, enjoying the power of their dreaming. The Pauline Oliveros Foundation in New York was founded with that vision in mind and it would become the Deep Listening Institute in Kingston, NY. Pauline and I worked hard and played hard to bring our dreaming into this reality. As it turned out, I was exploring dreams with my women's circles on the East Coast while Pauline was expressing her deep interest in dreams with her students, colleagues and women's circles during her years at the University of Southern California.

We formed the idea of a retreat in 1991, when our old friend Heloise Gold told us of her brother's small retreat place 8,000 feet high atop a mountain in New Mexico. 'Let's call it a Deep Listening Retreat,' Pauline suggested. I facilitated my Dream Awareness circles during the Deep Listening Retreats, which entailed a week or two weeks of living together without cell phones, eating vegetarian meals, sleeping in tents or raised platforms, surrounded by whispering Aspens. The concept of 'Twenty-four-hour Listening' emerged as we learned to deeply listen in our dreams. We created performances, compositions and rituals and became proficient in incubation, seeking specific information from our dreaming selves. We were freed from automatic sound exchanges with our companions in the mornings and experienced mornings or full days of being non-verbal. We began to experience Quantum Listening as we practised listening with simultaneous focal and global attention, also called exclusive and inclusive listening.

On the mountain, we came to understand that we are always dreaming, day and night. We experienced the expansion of our previously limited conception of 'dream', allowing for the quantum level of dreaming in which the barriers of communication were eased, and a Dream Community could flourish. On our morning walks, and during our evening circles, over lunch and during nap times, we maintained a simultaneous awareness of our individual dreaming with awareness of the Big Dream.

*

This dream continues to expand. Heloise wrote to Pauline after the 2001 retreat: 'I had a dream of you. You said that at the moment of death, we hear every single sound in the universe. You said, it is the most extraordinary sound. As you were describing it, I said I understood what you were saying and that I could see the sound as colours.'

In 2009, Pauline's dream on Rose Mountain expressed a lifelong concern: 'I see a woman in white on a mountain peak releasing white doves to fly over the world for peace.'

Notes

1. Joseph Chilton Pearce, *The Biology of Transcendence*, Park Street Press, 2002.
2. Fred Alan Wolf, *The Dreaming Universe*, Simon & Schuster, 1994.
3. Starhawk, *Dreaming the Dark: Magic, Sex, and Politics*, Beacon Press, 1982.
4. Dr Harold Rau, Institute of Medical Psychology, University of Tubingen.
5. Arthur Mindell, *Quantum Mind and Healing: How to Listen and Respond to Your Body's Symptoms*, Hampton Roads, 2004.

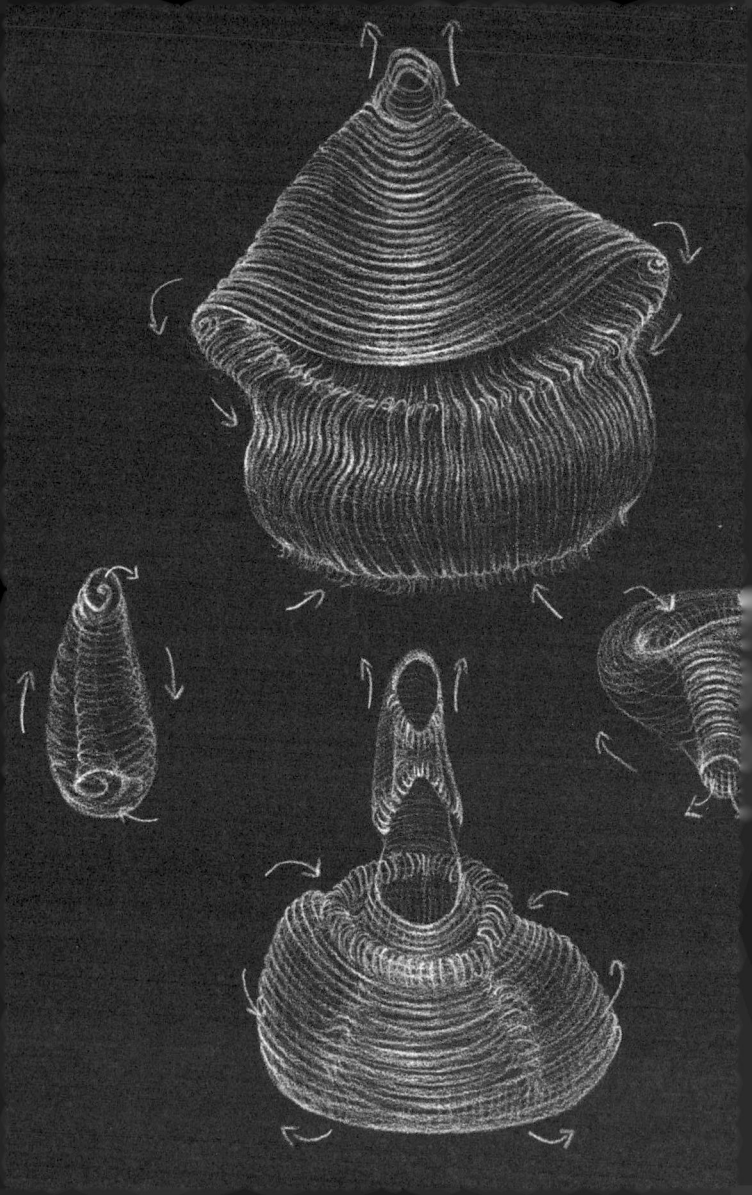

Afterword

North

BY SARAH SHIN

The sun is waiting for you to come back. Past the veil of skin, the light is tinged with blue and yellow. Although you want to stay, it's time to walk towards the bridge and return to day.

*

The message arrived before sleep broke – wordless, a secret seed. *We are to make a commitment to this world.*

Although the story constantly branches like a tree, like the tiny vessels I could see through the skin of my legs, what came through was: a commitment. To this world, this vessel, this body. This living archive – our memory of images accumulated over time. And what are we to do with that?

The morning light filled the room with openness. Possibility.

There was no moon in the cold sky when we left. A time for planting. The industrial labyrinth was also empty; tools, wheelbarrows, detritus and carts stood where they had been left in the narrow alleyways. It was our favourite neighbourhood, the oldest in the city where it felt like stepping into the past, when everyone must have dreamed. The building with the green light, the one with fifty-seven steps, was where we were headed for the ritual. The bar was as deserted as everywhere else. We walked up the stairs, and the green light changed to a pinkish red. The higher we climbed, the deeper we went into ourselves until we reached the threshold. We stepped through the curtains and onto the stage of the theatre, where the play had already begun.

Act 1

Scene 1

S steps into the nocturnal building, concrete awash with green light, and climbs up fifty-seven steps over several flights. Some of the steps are stickered with: a ghost, an advert for a pizza delivery company, a basketball player wearing a jersey with the words 'just do it later'. Up the first flight, and down the landing, past the bar with a wreath on its door. Up the second, and to the upper private room. S opens the door. Four worldly leaders sit around a table laden with cash and jewellery. In the pink light, occasionally, their faces age by decades, centuries, just for a flash, before reverting to their usual personas: bored, arrogant, senile, blank. The Empress looks up from the table and directly at S.

Empress: You fool. It only begins when all has been lost.

Scene 2
Taking her place at the table, S falls asleep again, like a fool.

Act 2

Scene 1
From above, the mountain can be seen as a squared form with various pathways, within a circle with no beginning or end. The dark forest blanketing the foothills contains life and death. Here are the shadows that rise up to make themselves known; here is the green dome that contains the uncontainable – the green light heart network of infinite love. Here are the forces that appear to be opposites but in fact hold the other in the way that my body is

coiled into a circle, a snake eating its tail. In the dome, the plants are words, signifying. One plant opens like a flower to show itself: its body spells 'love'.

S: What if I put some characters in here, into the dream?

Wise Old Woman: She's woven threads of magic spells into it.

The old woman cuts a hole in S' chest and hides some earth in it.

Scene 2
When she wakes up, the wound is healing. The witch is a wise and beautiful old woman clothed in purple. She has let go of what forged her. She has been to the other side and come back.

S: We have met before, a long time ago but I cannot quite remember. You were there at the pyramids.

Wise Old Woman: Once a traveller followed my hand to this place, where images are born and made. It is necessary, sometimes, to grieve the loss of illusions. To go deeper into the dream.

Act 3

Scene 1

The dream station is a cosmogram. Its cardinal directions are past, present, future and eternity, each marked by an obelisk. When rung, they produce vibrations, wormholes, microtubules of consciousness – images. A girl falling among bells, each curve curving into another. A spinal energetic totem. Phantom wings, trailing roots. Ghost frequencies moving in and out of this dimension.

S: What is the map of the heart?

Oracle: It's in the fourth dimension, which expresses itself in time. And things can be inside and outside, like a tesseract. If three dimensions are *xyz*, the fourth is *u*.

S: You.

Oracle: Like the moon could be folded inside out
and that could be okay.
So I could pull myself inside out
and turn you outside in.

S: Are dreams the fourth dimension?

Oracle: In dreams, there's no three-dimensional space-time rules. It's quantum: particles can be entangled and in superposition on the level of consciousness. So yes, they could be the fourth dimension.

S: How do we get there?

Oracle: How we get there is by stopping believing in three-dimensional space-time.

S: From now on, I'm going to start walking into tables.

Oracle: You already do.

S rolls her eyes.

Scene 2

Taking a calligraphy brush, S draws the shape of the Great Egg on the floor of the dream station and consults the oracle again.

S: Okay, so what about the fifth dimension?

Oracle: I can't tell you that.

S: Why not?

Oracle: I just can't

S: If you can't explain the fifth dimension, how do people think there's up to ten?

Oracle: It comes out in mathematics.

S rolls her eyes again.

S: If the impossible mountain is north, the substance of dream is image, are we always dreaming our own birth?

*

I turned to face the audience and walked over the bridge. Backstage, the fourth act took place. Always returning to a conversation with god, the Big Dream, breaking open the spell of a world in which you and I are separate.

You do not need 'I' when the veil goes. Listen and let go.

The dreamer dreams that the dream is inside you and outside of you. The world folds into you. Commit to it.

> *She's woven threads of magic spells into it*
> *The way in is the way out*
> *Take my hand: it is a map*

Images by Sammy Lee

Cymatics Studies, 2025

- p.vii *Bell Slime Plants.*
- p.5 *Spinal Totem.*
- p.8 *Light Calligraphy.*
- p.15 *Tardigrade.*
- p.20 *Phantom Wings.*
- p.25 *Microtubular Wormholes.*
- p.30 *Ghost Frequency.*
- p.35 *Seed of Life.*
- p.44 *Force Lines.*

IONE is an author, playwright, director and an improvising text-sound artist. In addition to multiple performances internationally, she has created numerous large music theatre works with her creative partner and spouse, the composer Pauline Oliveros. IONE's memoir, *Pride of Family: Four Generations of American Women of Color*, was a New York Times Notable Book on its publication. She was artistic director of Deep Listening Institute for fifteen years and is currently a Deep Listening Consultant at the Centre for Deep Listening, Troy, NY. As founding director of the Ministry of Maât, IONE received the 2019 Arts Mid Hudson Individual Artists Award and a Certificate of Merit from the General Assembly of the State of New York, and was a member of the Kingston Arts Commission for several years. IONE's most recent opera, *TOUCH*, with composer Karen Power, premiered at Irish National Opera in 2021.

SAMMY LEE works across images, moving image, video games and spatial installation to create complex, visceral worlds. Her practice explores how ritual and technology offer forms of attunement amid the entropic force of the digital. Past works have traversed subjects such as K-pop and soft power, Korean shamanism and polyrhythm, cymatics and sonic geometry, memory palaces, metaphysical gaming, and the tarot. Her work has been shown internationally, including solo presentations: *Cornucopia* (Stephanie Kim Gallery, New York, 2024), *Mirror I: The Sea* (with Sarah Shin, SWAY, Barry, 2022), *Aviary* (Tate St Ives Commission, UK, 2021). Lee trained in architecture at the Architectural Association and in sculpture at the Royal College of Art, and now co-directs Standard Deviation, a multi-disciplinary collective exploring the coincidence of geometric, psychic and inhabited spaces. Lee lives and works in London.

SARAH SHIN explores dreams, myth, cosmic speculation and transformation through writing, research, publishing, curation and creation. Her current collaborations include: with Irene Revell, the book and curatorial project *Bodies of Sound*; with Sammy Lee, *Mirror*, a video game that journeys through a mythical world of correspondences; and Concrete Poetry with Mark Lowe. She is a founder of Silver Press, the feminist publisher, and Spiral House, a new imprint for art, poetry and ways of knowing; Ignota, the creative publishing and curatorial house (2018-2024); New Suns literary festival at the Barbican Centre; and Standard Deviation.